Original title:
The Tranquil Reef

Copyright © 2025 Creative Arts Management OÜ
All rights reserved.

Author: Evan Hawthorne
ISBN HARDBACK: 978-1-80587-272-6
ISBN PAPERBACK: 978-1-80587-742-4

Conversations with the Sea Floor

Bubbles rise up to say hello,
"You think you're clever, but I'm the show!"
The starfish giggles, clings to a rock,
"I'm not just a pretty face, I'm quite the talk!"

Coral chimed in with a splashy quirk,
"Why do fish swim? To find the best perk!"
Seahorses danced like they're at a ball,
"Just don't ask us to play football!"

A crab walked by in a sideways spree,
"I'm not lost, I'm just avoiding the sea!"
The octopus chuckled, inked up the tale,
"Life's just a game; I'll never go stale!"

The seaweed swayed with a blowfish grin,
"In this watery world, we're all kin!"
With a wave and a laugh, they all joined the fun,
Their underwater party had only begun!

The Calm Beneath the Surface

Fish in bright attire, do the twist,
They dance and they spin, can't resist.
Bubble-bursting laughter lifts the tide,
Seaweed sways along, with glee they glide.

Hushed Melodies of the Sea

Crabs on the sax, with a jazzy roam,
Clams play drums, creating a home.
Seahorses waltz with a splashy cheer,
While jellyfish jiggle, bringing good cheer.

Dive into Tranquility

Floating through waters, a turtle slow,
As fishes laugh at the weight of a glow.
An octopus juggles with quirky finesse,
Guests at the ball, wearing seaweed dress.

An Undersea Peace

Starfish lounging on a sandy chair,
They wear tiny hats, without a care.
Conch shells are gossiping, quite the scene,
Whispers of waves, a funny routine.

Beneath the Dappled Light

Bubbles rise with giggly glee,
Fish wear hats, just wait and see.
Corals dance in colors bright,
Underneath the dappled light.

Crabs with shades strut in style,
Sea turtles grinning all the while.
Whales hum tunes, not quite in key,
Here's the ocean's comedy!

The Whispering Sands of Time

Starfish gossip about the tide,
Laughing clownfish take a ride.
Seashells crack jokes, oh what a sight,
Rolling on the shore, delight!

Sea cucumbers know all the puns,
While dolphins play with beachside buns.
Seagulls squawk in laughter's rhyme,
Whispers float on waves of time.

A Palette of Calm

Anemones wave in the gentle breeze,
Jellyfish swirl with utmost ease.
Octopus joins in with squishy flair,
Painting joy in salty air.

Colorful fish can't help but dive,
In search of jokes they can't revive.
Life below, a canvas grand,
Smiles are drawn with expert hand.

Ocean's Quietude

In the reef, a snail tells tales,
Of ocean frolics and curious whales.
Seahorses prance, a classy parade,
Underwater antics, they've got it made!

Clownfish joke with impeccable wit,
While waving kelp plays a side split.
Every bubble bursts with glee,
In this calm, silly jubilee!

Whispers Beneath the Waves

In the depths where fish do chat,
They gossip on a pebble mat.
A crab in glasses tries to see,
While shrimp conclude, 'He's still crabby!'

Bubbles rise with ticklish glee,
The seaweed laughs, 'Come dance with me!'
Octopus sings in silly tones,
As clownfish mock in silly zones.

Colors of Stillness

A puffer fish with bumps in tow,
Claims he's a beauty, 'Just watch me glow!'
A turtle rolls its sleepy eyes,
And mutters, 'That's no great surprise.'

Bright starfish stretching on the sand,
Pretend to be the biggest band.
They play on waves, a surfy beat,
While seahorses tap their tiny feet.

Secrets of the Coral Garden

In the jungle of colors, they always tease,
A parrotfish munches, 'Oh, thank you, please!'
The sea urchins roll their spiky eyes,
'We're the bouncers, we know no lies!'

Jellyfish waltz, all twirly and free,
Swaying like dancers in a sea spree.
A clam just snickers, 'Don't be so shy,
Join our party, we'll all say hi!'

Serenity in Silken Waters

The sunlit waves all giggle and sway,
As fish flip silly in a splashy play.
A dolphin whispers, 'Did you see that flip?'
While a lazy seal takes his lunchtime sip.

Barnacles dressed in their fancy suits,
Claim they are the best, oh what a hoot!
In this calm place where laughter flows,
Even the sea cucumbers strike jolly poses.

Conversations with Sea Anemones

I asked an anemone, what's your day job?
It said, 'Tickling fish, I'm quite the mob!'
With tentacles wiggling, it sparked great cheer,
'Just don't call me late, I've a meeting near!'

The clownfish chimed in, making jokes all day,
'Your hair's quite a mess, did you swim in clay?'
They laughed and they danced in a salty ballet,
Together in bubbles, in a bright, fishy way.

Chasing Sunlit Shadows

Nibbling at seaweed, I see shadows sway,
'Is that a fish or just me, feeling gay?'
One starfish replied with a wink in its eye,
'Don't worry, my friend, it's just the tide nigh.'

With sunbeams above, we glimmer and glide,
Fish darting like thoughts, can't hide, can't abide!
'Who's faster?' we argue, in a playful race,
But the winner just swims away, quick as space.

Nature's Underwater Sanctuary

In a coral cathedral, I stopped for a snack,
Met a crab with a smile, and a tiny top hat!
'Care for a dance?' it said, with a cheery clap,
'Let's shell-abrate life, and not take a nap!'

A school of bright fish joined in the fun,
Twisting and turning, shimmering under the sun.
They formed a conga line, what a sight to behold,
Underwater parties, far more fun than gold!

Embracing the Abyss

In the depths where it's dark, I found quite the thrill,
A grouper named George with a dad joke to spill.
'Why don't we ever tell secrets to the sea?'
'Because it's too deep, it'll just laugh at thee!'

With laughter we swirled, in our own little whirl,
While drifting through currents, our fins gave a twirl.
Embracing the abyss, where the funny fish float,
Life's a wild ocean, with laughs as our boat!

Palette of the Deep Blue

In a world where fish dance bright,
They twirl and spin without a fright.
A crab in shades of neon green,
Wears a tiny hat, quite the scene!

The octopus, with flair so grand,
Plays the piano with each hand.
His jellyfish friends play back-up hums,
While starfish tap with their little thumbs.

The Soft Touch of Sea Breezes

Bubbles rise like giggles in the tide,
As seagulls swoop, they take a ride.
A clam tries to sing but pouts,
Says, "I'm no diva, no doubts!"

The seaweed sways, a wig of green,
Bobbed heads swaying, oh what a scene!
The sea cucumbers roll with glee,
Laughing at fish, 'Come swim with me!'

Moments in Aquatic Stillness

Corals lounge in their comfy beds,
While mackerels giggle, flipping heads.
A turtle snores, oh what a sound,
Even the sea horses gather 'round!

The darned lobster plays peek-a-boo,
With his prize-winning, red-shelled crew.
Underwater, it's all quite a joke,
As the shy fish giggle and poke.

Harmony of the Watery Realm

Beneath the waves where all seems sweet,
Clown fish joke about their feet.
A dolphin whistles funny tunes,
While octopuses juggle spoons!

The angelfish take selfies at dawn,
And huddle close till the light's gone.
With coral reefs as their backdrop bright,
They laugh and dance until the night.

Seafoam Serenade

Underwater giggles float like air,
A crab with a hat does a silly stare.
Starfish dancing, what a sight,
Even the jellyfish feels quite light.

A dolphin wore glasses to read the tide,
While turtles chuckled, they couldn't hide.
Seashells whisper secrets from the sand,
Like a clam with a joke, it's quite well planned.

Whirlpools swirl with laughter's delight,
As fish share punchlines in the moonlight.
Every wave carries a playful tune,
Under the sea, humor's in bloom.

Soothing Currents of Nature

Waves crash softly like a child's laugh,
A seahorse prances, strikes a pose for half.
Fish in bow ties dance on the floor,
While seaweed sways begging for more.

The otters play tag, rolling in glee,
Shells are their trophies, they can't agree!
An octopus juggles with eight silly hands,
While the crab critiques all his wild plans.

Bubble-blowing dolphins put on a show,
Wiggling their tails, they steal the flow.
Nature's a circus beneath the sun,
Every splash hints laughter's the main fun.

An Oasis of Corals

Corals giggle in colors so bright,
Hosting a party under the moonlight.
Anemones dance with a zany flare,
While clownfish chuckle, unaware of despair.

A parrotfish sings off-key in the blue,
Sardines form choirs, though one forgot the cue.
Lobsters in tuxedos searching for bling,
Every shell's a treasure, let the laughter ring.

Crabs play cards while wagging their claws,
But lose every time, oh what a cause!
Seashells giggle, echo the fun,
In this vibrant kingdom, laughter's a pun.

Deep Blue Reflections

In waters that shimmer, the antics abound,
A fish wearing sneakers is seen all around.
Turtles in glasses read the ocean map,
And prepare for a picnic—what a laugh trap!

A pufferfish jokes, 'Look, I'm not so bright!'
But balloons of air keep it soaring quite right.
The sea urchins chuckle as they roll on the floor,
Their prickly humor leaves everyone wanting more.

Among the seaweed, a fish plays the clown,
Wearing a crown made of kelp, floating down.
Jellyfish drift, their tentacles sway,
In this vast ocean, it's a funny ballet.

Undercurrent of Gentle Whispers

Bubbles bounce like giggling fish,
Coral hides, granting every wish.
A crab does the cha-cha on the sand,
While a seahorse claims the day, quite grand.

Anemones wave in a soft breeze,
Jellyfish dance with elegant ease.
Clownfish recreate grand mimicry,
In this underwater symphony, oh me!

Starfish play cards, on a dark rock,
While sea turtles ensure the clock.
The parrotfish snack on mac 'n cheese,
In a world that aims to please with great ease.

But watch for the octopus wearing a hat,
He thinks he's dapper, imagine that!
With laughter echoing in sun-drenched caves,
In the depths of the ocean, where humor waves.

The Peace of Ocean's Embrace

Waves serenade with a gentle hum,
As dolphins frolic, sounding like drums.
A fish in a tux gives a grand speech,
While sea cucumbers silently reach.

Turtles compete in a slow-motion race,
Adjusting their shells with elegant grace.
The clownfish grumble, arguing who's best,
In this peaceful place, never a jest.

Sea stars lounge, reading the news,
While hermit crabs pick the fanciest shoes.
The pufferfish poofs just for a laugh,
While schools of fish swim in perfect half.

Eels throw a party with seaweed treats,
Inviting the creatures, oh what a feat!
In their blue world, with swirls of delight,
A quirky reef, shining ever so bright.

Murmurs Beneath the Chaos

Coral reefs giggle, tickled by tides,
Where fish play tag, oh what joy abides!
A lionfish struts in dazzling fins,
While the octopus plans his next wins.

Sea urchins laugh at the shells they've worn,
While snails claim fashion as their sworn.
Dolphins dive in somersault glee,
Whispering secrets made just for me.

Bubbles burst, like giggles in air,
As flatfish camouflage, unaware.
They're so busy snoozing under the sun,
That no one thinks hiding could be such fun.

Even starfish join in on the joke,
As they twirl around like a merry folk.
With every wave and swirl of foam,
This lively scene feels just like home.

Enchantment of a Quiet Lagoon

In a lagoon where laughter swells,
The fish start telling their fishy tales.
An old turtle shares with a wink,
How he once swam with a mighty pink.

The plankton dance in flashy displays,
While seahorses tango in vibrant ways.
A shrimp with glasses reads the news,
In this tranquil place where nobody snooze.

With soft plumes of seaweed swaying low,
The flounders play peek-a-boo, what a show!
Starfish selling snacks, oh what a find,
In a market of humor, laughter aligned.

Their underwater disco lights up the night,
Where eels twist and turn, a delightful sight.
Bubble blowers create crowns of glee,
In this charming lagoon, carefree and free.

A Tapestry of Peace and Plankton

Fishes giggle in the tide,
Coral castles, where they hide.
Anemones wave, what a scene,
A jellyfish trips on marine cuisine.

Crabs do the cha-cha, oh so spry,
With seaweed hats, they wave goodbye.
Starfish twirl, what a sight,
Bubbles laugh in the soft moonlight.

Octopus juggling shells with flair,
A clownfish jokes, 'What's the fare?'
Lobsters sing a crustacean song,
In this underwater, quirky throng.

They swim in style, no care in the world,
With snappy gestures, their tentacles swirled.
A tranquil bubble, a hilarious fowl,
In the sea's embrace, all laugh and howl.

The Enchanted Seascape

Under waves where humor thrives,
A pelican busts out its jives.
Seahorses dance with tiny steps,
While sardines form a fishy prep.

Clownfish giggle, 'What's the deal?'
As they spin and they squeal.
Turtles wear their sunglasses proud,
The ocean's laughter, oh so loud.

Urchins chuckle, lost in thought,
They tell tales of battles fought.
With crabs that trot on sandy floors,
And dolphins who open giggling doors.

Corals blushing, colors bright,
With every wave, they spark delight.
In this realm of vibes so bright,
Laughter echoes, a joyful flight.

Symphony of the Submerged

In depths where giggles reverberate,
A whale hums tunes to celebrate.
Fish in top hats, quite the sight,
Breakdance to currents, such sheer delight.

Snails on surfboards, shy and meek,
Riding the waves, a cheeky streak.
With barnacles busting moves so sly,
They twirl and swirl and wave goodbye.

A goggle-eyed grouper claims the floor,
Singing ballads of ocean lore.
While dolphins share their witty banter,
Creating waves of laughs, none can slander.

As sea turtles join the groove,
With graceful spins, they make us move.
Nature's laughter from every side,
In this aquatic joy ride!

Dreamcatcher of the Deep

In shadowed depths where dreams are spun,
A clam whispers, 'Let's have some fun!'
With angles quirky and rhythm odd,
An oyster jokes, 'Oh, I'm a god!'

Pufferfish puffing on a thrill,
Claim their crown with perfect skill.
Bubble-blowers with silly tricks,
A colorful show, no need for picks.

Sea cucumbers trying to dance,
Gave the anemones a second chance.
With dingleberries swaying low,
In this whimsy, the laughter grows.

A driftwood stage for the stars to shine,
As fishy comedians softly dine.
In this dreamworld where giggles seep,
All find a laugh, from big to deep.

Echoes of Silent Currents

Bubbles rise like laughter, bright,
As fish chase tails in sheer delight.
The seaweed sways with a giggle's grace,
While crabs do the cha-cha, quicken the pace.

Coral castles hide and seek,
In this underwater hideaway unique.
With starfish stuck in pondering pose,
They wonder why their cousin's nose glows.

Dolphins play tag, flipping with flair,
While turtles just nod, too cool to care.
A jellyfish twirls in a wobbly dance,
Catching waves as they take a chance.

Whale songs echo like silly tunes,
Drifting softly beneath bright moons.
Sea urchins chuckle in spiky glee,
As the ocean spreads its humor free.

Colors of Peaceful Waters

In the depths, a rainbow plays,
With fish dressed up for grand parades.
Anemones wave to the passing schools,
While clownfish tease, those little fools.

Seahorses ride on bubbles' backs,
As octopuses plot their colorful hacks.
Porcupine fish puff up in fright,
As they think they're knights in armor bright.

A starry night under the sea,
With critters dancing wildly, carefree.
The corals giggle in yellow and blue,
As the waves tickle secrets, known to few.

A hermit crab shifts homes like a hat,
Saying, "This shell is nice, but that one's a cat!"
With laughter swirling in waters so deep,
The colors of joy make the ocean leap.

Meditative Tides

Waves whisper secrets, soft like a joke,
As seafoam giggles, rising and bespoke.
The sand dollars scatter, trying to hide,
While sea turtles nod, enjoying the ride.

Sylvan seaweed sways, it's quite the sight,
Ballet of bubbles that dance with delight.
Clownfish chuckle, with friends in rhyme,
Gossiping sea tales, while passing the time.

Gentle ripples share tales of the day,
While pirate fish scurry, pretending to play.
A sandpiper prances on sifting grains,
As seagulls play tag, warming their veins.

Meditative moments flow like a stream,
Where fish swim in circles, living the dream.
And in this calm, funny tides do twist,
Serenity reigns, with a cheeky tryst.

Lullabies of the Ocean Floor

The ocean hums a cozy tune,
To starfish snuggled by the light of the moon.
Eels wriggle to sleep, wrapped in seaweed,
As clownfish book club starts with great speed.

Gentle waves rock sleepy sand, oh so slow,
While jellyfish dream of putting on a show.
A hermit crab hums as he cheekily creeps,
Poking fun at the barnacles stuck in heaps.

Whales croon lullabies to the moon's glow,
While dolphins dive down with a laugh and a flow.
Sleepy scallops flutter their shells with delight,
Drifting off, snuggled in the watery night.

In the depths where silence softly roars,
Funny fish share tales of life's grand tours.
As shadows dance lightly, and dreams start to soar,
The lullabies keep flowing, forevermore.

The Stillness Between Waves

In a world where fish wear hats,
Dancing lightly on their mats.
A crab in glasses reads a book,
While all the seaweed comes to look.

The starfish throws a tea party grand,
With jellybeans from a distant land.
The bubbles giggle, float and pop,
As sea cucumbers do a hop.

A dolphin sings a silly tune,
While octopuses juggle by the moon.
The reef's full of laughter, a sight to see,
In this kingdom beneath the salty sea.

So come along, don't delay,
Join in the fun, let's laugh and play.
In the depths, where the silliness thrives,
Every creature has their fun-filled lives.

Echoes in the Soft Sand

On the shore, a hermit crab trudges along,
With a shell that sings its own silly song.
The gulls all laugh, their wings spread wide,
At the antics of the sand, which tries to hide.

A clam tells tales of treasures near,
While sea turtles race, showing no fear.
The sandcastle stands proud, wearing a crown,
Until a wave comes and knocks it down.

Starfish giggles, giving a wink,
As they compete in who blinks the quickest, I think.
With each splash, the tide's got a joke,
While sea urchins giggle, their spines all awoke.

In the soft embrace of grains so fine,
Where laughter echoes, and sea breezes shine.
Adventure awaits, come take a stand,
Join the spectacle on this funny strand.

Luminescent Dreams in Quiet Waters

Beneath the waves where glowfish dart,
A seahorse spins, an underwater art.
The jellyfish dance, with lights that flick,
While clams perform a magic trick.

In the calm, where secrets gleam,
A narwhal brews a bubble team.
With luminous tails, they frolic and play,
In this radiant spot where laughter holds sway.

The seaweed sways, a green-haired queen,
Hosting a ball, oh, what a scene!
With each flicker, they share a laugh,
As the sea stars join for a silly giraffe.

So glide alongside the glowing crew,
For under the surface, there's fun for you.
In waters deep, where the light does gleam,
Let's chase the shadows, and dream a dream.

The Solace of Sea Gods

High tides don't need a throne,
When a crab king rules the ocean's zone.
His scepter's made of shiny shells,
While fish joke about the bloopers they tell.

The dolphins play hopscotch with waves,
While sea urchins hide in their caves.
A mermaid with a talent for pun,
Tells tales of the sea that's always fun.

The seadragons in a parade,
With colors so bright, an artful cascade.
The sea foam giggles, rolls on the shore,
"Was that a wave or a lion's roar?"

So heed the call of the ocean's jest,
Join the revelry, let the waves be blessed.
In this watery reminiscence, we find the key,
To the solace that binds the wild, free sea.

Ribbons of Cool Waters

Bubbles rise like birthday cheer,
While fish dance, with not a fear.
Octopus wears a party hat,
And all the crabs are having a spat.

Starfish play hide and seek,
Pufferfish puff, looking sleek.
The seaweed sways, quite the sight,
As dolphins leap with sheer delight.

A clam tries to tell a joke,
But it's shell-shocked and goes up in smoke.
Everyone laughs till they turn blue,
In these cool waters, oh so true.

With jellyfish throwing a rave,
The ocean floor is quite the cave.
Come join the fun and take a dive,
In these ribbons where we feel alive.

Tranquility Underneath

Seahorses wear their finest ties,
While fish gossip with big, round eyes.
The coral crew throws a picnic bash,
But the jellybeans keep making a splash.

Clams attempt to whistle a tune,
While bubbles burst like a balloon.
A grouchy crab grumbles with a sigh,
He lost his lunch to a passing fly.

The turtles tell tales, old and grand,
About treasure maps and a far-off land.
Fish are jealous; they want that fame,
But no one wins at this silly game.

Oh! Here comes a shark in disguise,
With a wig and enormous eyes.
The fish giggle with sheer delight,
In this peaceful realm, everything's right.

A Symphony in Blue

Underwater, a conductor stands tall,
With starfish playing the marimba, oh what a ball!
Anemones swaying, a delicate dance,
While clownfish prance in a jolly trance.

Krill make up the bright little choir,
Encouraging bubbles to pop and retire.
The sea anemones sway to the beat,
As snails applaud with tiny little feet.

The concert begins with a grand old whale,
Who sings so loud, it raises the sail.
Everyone claps, even the rock,
As the funny fish all dance round the clock.

When the jam ends with a splashy grand finale,
A crab makes sure it's quite a silly rally.
They all bow down with a splash and a sway,
In their symphony, they'll always play.

Where Silence Meets the Sea

In still waters where the fish make friends,
The gossip travels, never ends.
A turtle sighs, just taking a break,
While shrimp argue about their next cake.

The sea cucumbers lounge in a row,
With sea urchins discussing the show.
Each wave that passes brings new chatter,
Like seahorses debating what really matters.

A clownfish takes center stage, you know,
Pulls funny faces, putting on a show.
Laughter bubbles up, rising fast,
In this quiet spot, fun unsurpassed.

And while the waves play a gentle tune,
The starfish giggles beneath the moon.
With peace in laughter, they do decree,
That fun and silence dance beautifully.

Pondering the Depths of Calmness.

In waters blue, the fish do prance,
They wiggle and giggle in a silly dance.
A crab in a tux, with a bowtie neat,
Claims he's the king, oh what a feat!

The starfish plays poker, on the ocean bed,
While the octopus chuckles, wearing a hat on his head.
Seahorses sip tea, gossiping away,
They laugh at seaweed, in their funny sway.

A turtle's slow waltz brings joy to the view,
While jellyfish float, like balloons in a zoo.
'What's for dinner?' the dolphin will shout,
'Sushi party tonight! Get ready, no doubt!'

So ponder beneath the waves all around,
Where laughter and fun, in the currents abound.
Just keep swimming and smile, as you glide through the blue,
In this underwater carnival, with antics anew.

Whispers of Coral Dreams

In the coral grove, secrets are shared,
Clams crack jokes, and the shrimp are prepared.
The anemones sway, putting on a show,
While the clownfish laughs, in their colorful glow.

A seahorse recites, a poem so bold,
Of treasure lost, and legends told.
The pufferfish grins, puffing with pride,
In the secretive realms where silliness hides.

Bubbles and giggles, tickles in tow,
As the grouper does pirouettes, swaying to and fro.
The sea cucumbers chuckle, their humor right deep,
While the eel tells a tale that makes the sea weep.

In this whimsical world, where wonders beam,
With laughter and joy, fulfilling the dream.
So dive into laughter, where the fun's so supreme,
In the gentle embrace of aquatic esteem.

Serenity Beneath Waves

Under the surface, where the silliness flows,
The fish wear their sunglasses, striking cool poses.
A dolphin plays tag with a flailing old boot,
While a sea turtle giggles, giving chase to that loot.

Beneath the still waves, a party unfolds,
With conch shell trumpets and stories retold.
An octopus juggles with a watch and a sock,
While sea bass tap dance on a ticklish rock.

The barnacles boast of their beauty so grand,
As the starfish debates, 'Who's the best in the band?'
The lobsters complain, about butter and bread,
While a clown in the sea feels it's best left unsaid.

So find the calmness, in laughter and jest,
Beneath the soft blue, where the joy feels the best.
In this playful kingdom, the mirth never waives,
Join in the laughter, in the peace of the waves.

Harmony in Aquatic Depths

In the depths of the sea, where the water's a balm,
A fish tells a riddle, his demeanor quite calm.
The shrimp high-fives an octopus friend,
As a whale cracks a joke, with joy to extend.

Amidst all the chaos, there's laughter profound,
With schools of bright fish, swirling around.
A grouper wears glasses, looking quite smart,
While a pirate's lost parrot plays music to part.

The sea anemones giggle, in colorful dives,
While crabs do the limbo, showing their jives.
Each current a promise, each wave a delight,
In the harmony found, beneath the moonlight.

So let's dive into joy, where the humor grows deep,
With tales of the sea, that swim into sleep.
For laughter is treasure, and fun's always cheap,
In the depths of the calm, where memories keep.

Reflections of a Forgotten Tide

Bubbles bounce like giggling friends,
Fish wear hats, their laughter blends.
Octopus tries to juggle shells,
But drops them all, oh what befells!

Coral castles, bright and neat,
Crabs dance on with tiny feet.
Seahorses twirl, a sight so grand,
While starfish clap, just as they planned.

A whale sneezes, what a sound,
Echoes through the sea around.
With each wave, the antics soar,
Oh, the sea, who could want more?

The Dance of Sunlit Depths

In the depths where sunlight plays,
Fishes dance in joyful rays.
Clownfish giggle in their mime,
Silly moves, it's showtime!

Anemones wave, 'Come on in,'
While shrimps prepare their spicy din.
Turtles twirl with such delight,
As bubbles burst and take to flight.

Gobies hide, then peek with glee,
Playing hide and seek, can't you see?
Amidst the waves, the fun won't stop,
In this world, we jump and hop!

The Calm Before the Reef

A gentle wave rolls in for tea,
A hippo joins, oh what a spree!
Manta rays glide, look so prime,
In the calm, let's have a rhyme.

Shrimp are flipping pancakes fast,
A feast awaits, we're having a blast.
Eels sneak in for a snooze or two,
While jellyfish paint the ocean blue.

The sea anemone stifles a yawn,
Says, "I'll wake up with the dawn!"
Then suddenly, the party's on,
In this bliss, laughter's never gone!

Beneath the Surface of Time

Clocks tick slowly under the sea,
Where mermaids sip their herbal tea.
An octopus reads a funny book,
While fishes gather for a look.

Shrimps play cards, risk it all,
A tiny crab stands proud and tall.
Betting shells, the stakes are high,
"Raise the stakes!" is the joyful cry!

But when the tide begins to roll,
The laughter fades, it takes a toll.
Yet soon again, the fun will climb,
As we dive down, beneath the rhyme!

Sanctuary of Serene Waves

In a world of fins and tails,
Fish gossip behind the coral veils.
Octopi play hide and seek,
Crabs dance, yet they don't speak.

Anemones sway like they're groovin',
With starfish having an all-day movin'.
Seahorses trot in their sweet parade,
While turtles munch on seaweed made.

Jellyfish glow like disco lights,
Throwing a party on silent nights.
With laughter bubbling through the deep,
They mingle where the secrets keep.

So come dive in, enjoy the show,
With every splash, let your bliss grow!
Where laughter echoes with each wave,
And every marine friend, is quite brave.

The Poetry of Coral Bowers

Coral trees with stories abound,
Where fish line up, all gathered round.
A zebrafish shares a joke so bright,
While sea cucumbers giggle with delight.

Pufferfish puffed, looking so grand,
Claiming their spot in bubbles they planned.
Clownfish chuckling at their own fate,
"Why stay home? This place is first-rate!"

Shrimp writes poems on sandy scrolls,
As dolphins spin and dive with roles.
An octopus gestures with a flair,
While turtles giggle without a care.

So inside this reef, both calm and fun,
Every creature shines like the sun.
In the depths of the ocean's disguise,
Lies humor wrapped in watery ties.

Dreaming Beneath the Salty Skies

Bubbles rise like dreams afloat,
As fish don hats made of seaweed tote.
Starfish lounge in their sandy beds,
While seahorses exchange silly threads.

A dolphin swims by with a broad grin,
Singing off-key, it's a laugh to begin!
Clams snap shut at a crab's quick pun,
Even the sea stars start a punny run.

With every wave, silly tales unwind,
Unseen giggles from treasures combined.
"Why don't fish play cards?" is the tease,
"Because they're afraid of the deck, you see!"

In this realm where laughter prevails,
With friends who share amusing tales.
Beneath those skies with salty smiles,
Happiness swims for countless miles.

Gentle Currents, Quiet Retreats

Beneath the waves where the fish thrive,
Bubble machines make bubbles alive.
Clownfish wear noses, far too bright,
While whales throw parties in sheer delight.

Pipefish twirl like a concert star,
With jellyfish spinning, oh what a bazaar!
Crabs upchuck because of their catch,
Leaving pearls that scratch their own patch.

Anemones wave as if they know,
How to dance in currents, a gentle flow.
With laughter whispering against coral walls,
Each echoing giggle softly calls.

So here, where the playful waters play,
All creatures find a wacky day.
In stillness, humor cleverly creeps,
As oceanic secrets the deep sea keeps.

Veils of Gentle Light

In the ocean's quilt of blue,
Jellyfish dance with a silly hue,
They glow and sway like a nightlight,
As fish chuckle, what a sight!

Turtles wear their shells too tight,
Claiming they're dashing, oh what a fright!
They slide and glide like a slippery bowl,
While the crabs wave, 'We control the shoal!'

Seahorses prance in comical rows,
With tiny laughs that no one knows,
Flipping their fins in choreographed glee,
Saying, "Catch us if you can, that's the key!"

Anemones tickle and tease the fish,
"Oh look, it's breakfast—make a wish!"
But the fish just giggle and swim away,
In this deep sea circus, they play all day.

The Breath of Forgotten Shores

A clam makes jokes; it's quite absurd,
With pearls so shiny, it starts to stir,
"Why do they call me a shellfish brat?
I'm just guarding treasures; how about that?"

The coral houses a band of shrimp,
Doing a jig with a tiny limp,
"Two steps left and a twirl to the right,
Let's rock the sea floor till the morning light!"

Octopus dreams in a splashy disguise,
Dressing up like a fisherman's prize,
"Tell me the secret to hook and reel,
I'd rather dance than be someone's meal!"

Starfish giggle with their pointy rays,
Counting all the laughs from yesterday,
In the depths of the sea there's always fun,
With every wave, new jokes are spun!

Guardians of the Whispering Tide

A seagull swoops with a cheeky grin,
"Hey fish friends, have you heard the din?
It's the tide's gossip, swirling and free,
About a crab who thinks he's a marquee!"

An old turtle snores on a rock with pride,
While starfish practice their graceful glide,
"Let's add some flair, a twist of the tail,
To impress the sharks in our next grand sale!"

The anglerfish grins with a glowing bait,
"Come closer, come closer, I'll give you a plate!"
But the fishes just giggle, "We're wise to your game,
We'd rather swim free than end up in fame!"

Bubble-blowing fish create a tune,
That dances with tides under the moon,
Together they laugh, with scales that shine bright,
In this watery world, they find pure delight!

Illuminations in a Hidden World

In the depths where the colors ignite,
A clownfish juggles, what a delight!
With bubbles and laughs in every flip,
"Come join the show; don't let it slip!"

A conch shell hums a bubbly song,
While the shrimps tap dance all night long,
"Oysters shush, this is our grand fight,
To see who's the silliest—what's your light?"

Watch out for the dolphins, so spry,
Who tell tall tales of pies in the sky,
"Did you hear about the whale's big surprise?
He wanted to dance but just floats, how wise!"

In every crevice, joy never wanes,
With laughter and twirls, it flows through the veins,
In this magical realm, the fun never ends,
As currents weave stories between sea friends.

A Garden of Aquatic Serenity

Bubbles rise in a dance, so bright,
Fish wearing hats hide out of sight.
Coral castles hold court with glee,
While crab chefs prepare a feast for three.

Seaweed sways like it's at a ball,
Jellyfish trip—oh, they take a fall!
An octopus juggles with flair so bold,
While snails tell tales that never get old.

Starfish play chess on a grand old stone,
They strategize moves, all alone.
With a wink, seahorses twirl and spin,
In this underwater world, all can win.

The clownfish giggle, tucked in their nook,
Plotting their pranks like pages in a book.
And if you listen, you will find,
The ocean whispers—so kind, so blind.

Traces of the Unseen

In shadows swim the giggling eels,
Showing off their slippery deals.
Pufferfish puff, round as a balloon,
While shrimp start breakdancing to a tune.

The hidden crabs, all dressed in style,
Wave their claws in a sassy smile.
In the depths, the pranks never end,
Even the seashells around the bend.

Ghostly fish with a sense of grace,
Swirl through currents, oh, what a race!
They vanish, reappear with glee,
Playing hide and seek like it's not a spree.

And when the moon grins down so wide,
The sea life laughs, no need to hide.
Echos of giggles drift through the blue,
In a realm where the strange feels true.

The Breath of Liquid Light

Sunbeams dance on the watery floor,
As wise old turtles stop to explore.
Zooming fish show off their flair,
Like underwater athletes with some air.

With glittering scales like confetti so bright,
They wiggle and giggle, oh, what a sight!
Anemones sway, forming noodle-like chains,
While clownfish engage in hilarious games.

The sea cucumbers mimic a walk,
While dolphins joke with a flip and a talk.
Bubbles burst with laughter and cheer,
As corals gossip—we can overhear!

In the depths where joy never sinks,
An aquarium of jokes, or so one thinks.
The ocean ponders in waves so light,
Finding humor in each little bite.

Visions in Wandering Current

Currents carry the tales of old,
Of sunken ships and treasures bold.
Starfish ponder with a look so sly,
As sea turtles surf as time goes by.

The anglerfish shines a light so dim,
Making friends with a blobfish whim.
They gather for tea by the seaweed green,
Discussions of dreams that drift between.

Anemones giggle at passing fish,
Throwing sea parties with a grand swish.
In the dance of the waves, laughter spins,
As even the mollusks enjoy their spins.

In a realm where currents intertwine,
The aquatic antics shine brightly and fine.
Dancing through waters, friends gather near,
In a world where laughter holds no fear.

Where Silence Meets the Sea

Bubbles rise, fish laugh and dance,
A clownfish slips, gives us a glance.
Coral bed, a vibrant parade,
Starfish lounge, in sunlight they wade.

Octopus wears a top hat so grand,
He juggles pearls, isn't it planned?
A sea turtle glides, all cool and sly,
He takes a selfie, with a wink and a eye.

Little shrimp wearing shoes made of foam,
They strut and prance, like they're at home.
Seaweed sways with a giggling sound,
As jellyfish waltz all around.

So here we float, in laughter's embrace,
The ocean's a circus, a wild, funny place.
Fish tickle each other, they swim in delight,
In this watery world, everything feels right.

A Voyage to Underwater Stillness

Sailing downward, where the giggles reside,
With dolphins playing, they take us for a ride.
Sea cucumbers feel so out of place,
With their slow-motion wiggle, what a funny race!

Anemones waving with flair and style,
Look at those fish, they haven't seen sunshine in a while!
A crab with a beret, looking quite brash,
Attempts to recite some undersea trash.

Clams sing softly, a tune that they know,
As they snap their shells in a clammy show.
Eels peek out wearing a mask of surprise,
But they can't fool us—those sly little guys!

Under the waves, where laughter is keen,
Every fin and flip feels like a scene.
With our hearts light and spirits at play,
The ocean's a stage where we giggle away.

Murmurs of Marine Life

In deep waters where the whispers abound,
Fish share secrets, they gather around.
A pufferfish puffs, like a balloon in flight,
Giggling with pride at his comical sight.

Seahorses strut, a slow-motion race,
They bob and they weave, with a smile on their face.
Bubble-blowing contest, who'll be the champ?
The winner's a sea snail, looking quite damp.

An octopus tickles a friend with a tentacle,
While sharks tell jokes, oh so nonsensical.
A walrus clad in a velvet cape,
Hums a sea shanty, oh what a shape!

So beneath the waves, where laughter can bloom,
Marine life gathers to chase away gloom.
With each splash and giggle, the stories take flight,
In this realm of wonders, everything feels right.

Beneath the Blue Embrace

Beneath the waves, the silliness flows,
With fish in bow ties and clams in old clothes.
A daring hermit crab dashes in haste,
Lost in a shell, oh, what a waste!

Turtles glide through kelp, quite unbothered,
While sea stars lounge, laughing like they've got it all offered.
A dolphin plays tag with a floating sea sponge,
Creating a ruckus, where we all plunge.

The urchins giggle, in colorful spines,
Crafting jokes that are simply divine.
A grouper with glasses, all wise and astute,
Schmoozes with lobsters, sharing old loot.

In this babbling brook of salt and of cheer,
The moods are light, and the friendships are clear.
Here's to the sea, with its peculiar grace,
Where humor and joy find their perfect space.

A Sanctuary of Bright Echoes

Fish dance in bubbles, they laugh and they spin,
Coral plays ukulele, the party begins!
Anemones peek, with their hair all a-fluff,
They're the star of the show, just can't get enough.

Octopus jokes, they tickle the fins,
Turtles wear glasses, looking for wins.
Bubble-blowers giggle, making quite a scene,
Seaweed wigs waving, all a vibrant green.

Starfish claim they can shine, what a big boast,
"I can stick to the wall!" is their proudest toast.
Crabs throw a dance-off, with claws held so high,
Who knew that the sea could be so spry?

A clownfish joins in, with a nose so red,
Tickling their gills 'til they're dizzy and spread.
In this underwater giggle-fest, so bright,
Who knew sea life offered such pure delight?

Tales from the Depths of Blue

An eel with a smile found a tuba down there,
He started a band, with great seaweed flair.
Whales made a splash, turning waves into cheer,
Singing sea shanties with a pint of cold beer!

Squid tried to moonwalk but slipped on a shell,
Her buddies all chuckled, 'Oh dear, what the hell!'
They laughed till they rolled on the soft ocean floor,
Crabs joined the fun, and they danced for some more!

A dolphin named Gary wrote jokes for the crew,
With puns made of seaweed and laughs that just grew.
Seahorses swayed, with their tails on display,
In this salty fiesta, who needed a bay?

With harmonies rising, they floated with ease,
As jellyfish floated like batches of cheese.
In depths so enchanting, where life finds its groove,
These tales make the ocean the best place to move!

Meditations in Oceanic Echoes

Surrounded by bubbles, a lobster sits tall,
He meditates deeply on the coral wall.
Fish pass by giggling, "What's he thinking now?"
"I'm finding my center," he whispers, "and wow!"

An urchin named Morty tried yoga one day,
But failed with a twist, said, "I think I'll just stay!"
The clowns at the surface missed the zen in the blue,
Too busy doing flips, but they giggled, it's true!

The shells held a meeting, debating the waves,
"Should we go to the surface or stay in our caves?"
Their voices like whispers, a soft tide of jest,
Finding joy in the silence, they felt truly blessed.

Meanwhile, krill danced, tiny swirls in a trance,
Inviting all friends to the undersea dance.
Meditation's great, with laughter's sweet tone,
In this watery world, we're never alone!

In the Arms of the Sea

Oh, the sea gives a hug, with its waves oh-so-soft,
As fish play on guitars, they launch into loft.
Crabs in tuxedos enjoy a grand feast,
With plankton on plates, they're charming at least!

The sea cucumber sighed, "What a life that I lead,
No walking, no worries, just float with great speed!"
Clownfish announce, with a whimsical cheer,
"Don't forget our party, we'll make it a year!"

Dolphins dive deep, with flips and a grin,
Tickling the sea stars, letting joy in.
The mermaids all giggle, with hair of bright hue,
Crafting wild stories, as only they do!

In this watery wonderland, laughter abounds,
Every splash tells a tale, oh, what joy surrounds.
In the arms of the ocean, we dance without fee,
Life's a splash of fun, as wild as can be!

Confluences of Serenity

In the depths where fishes play,
Corals dance, a colorful ballet.
Starfish giggle on sandy beds,
Even crabs crack jokes, it spreads!

Anemones sway to a silent tune,
Turtle nods to the jellyfish moon.
Lobsters laugh, they're quite a sight,
With pinchers raised, they argue all night.

Clownfish swap tales of the day,
While octopus throws hints of dismay.
With wink and swirl, they jive and spin,
In this world, who could be grim?

Bubble-blowers boast their best,
"Watch my bubble, it's the greatest!"
Each pop a laugh, each glance a cheer,
In this cozy sea, all's clear!

An Underwater Reverie

Under the waves, a world so bright,
Fish wear smiles, such a funny sight.
Seaweed tickles with every flow,
While dolphins play tag, putting on a show.

There's a grouper that loves to sing,
Though off-key, he's the underwater king.
Shells echo laughter, some do boast,
About parties thrown by a wise old ghost.

Urchins roll by with spikes held high,
"Good day!" they shout, oh my, oh my!
With a wink and a nod, they pass on through,
While turtles enjoy a leisurely brew.

Clam chatter fills the salty air,
As seahorses flaunt their stylish flair.
In this jolly old reef where fun thrives,
Underwater giggles, oh how it jives!

Serene Colors of the Abyss

In the ocean's embrace where colors gleam,
Squids draft jokes like a comedic dream.
Each hue is vibrant, a capricious splash,
As fish share secrets in a watery bash.

The parrotfish laughs, munching coral soup,
While playful seals sing in a hilarious troupe.
Pufferfish stand guard, all puffed and proud,
"Careful now," they warn, "or we'll not let you crowd!"

Clownfish wiggle, with antics so bold,
Riding waves, they are never too old.
With a flick of a fin, they cause delight,
Bubbling giggles, a sparkling sight.

An array of wonders, quirks unfurl,
In this whimsical world, watch stories swirl.
With laughter and joy, each creature's a muse,
In the depths of the sea, there's much to amuse!

The Art of Water's Embrace

In crystal blue, the humor flows,
Where fins and flippers meet and pose.
A menagerie of fish, each with a grin,
Join in the dance, let the fun begin!

Bubbles rise like laughter bright,
Joining clams in a jovial fight.
They snap their shells, making quite the sound,
As giggles and glee drift all around.

The wise old turtle shares a tall tale,
About a seaweed that turned into a whale.
With every twist, the crowd does roar,
In this slice of life, who could ask for more?

Manta rays glide, casting shadows so wide,
While tiny fish hitch a ride, full of pride.
In this playful domain where laughter's embraced,
Through water's art, we bravely face!

Stillness Among Living Stones

In the quiet of the sea, stones sit in a line,
Holding underwater meetings, plotting whims divine.
Anemones whisper secrets, while crabs dance around,
Stones shrug off the gossip, never making a sound.

A starfish yawned aloud, proclaiming it a day,
Said, 'Why move, when the tide can carry me away?'
Clownfish giggled gently, in their coral recess,
While an octopus waved, dressing in sheer finesse.

A loggerhead took a nap, snoozing on a patch,
But jellyfish snickered softly, 'He's such a sleepy catch!'
Bubbles floated past him, a soft and shining tease,
Echoes of the laughter danced lightly on the breeze.

Those living stones just chuckled, beneath the water's glow,
In the sea where all are little, even the mighty flow.
With joy and ribbony waves, they play their gentle role,
In a world where stillness rocks, yet liveliness is whole.

Ballet of the Gentle Fins

Bubbles rise like curtains, as the fish take the stage,
In twirling, graceful motions, they perform a fine page.
Sardines glide in circles, a shiny silver bunch,
While seahorses whisper softly, 'Now it's time for lunch!'

A puffer fish, grand solo, inflates to fit the part,
While sea turtles cheer him on, with a warm and joyful heart.
An urchin rolls his eyes, 'Oh please, just keep it fun!'
Yet the dancing never falters, under rays of sun.

A wrasse twirls in the current, wearing bright and bold hues,
While parrotfish munch on corals, singing fishy blues.
The clownfish laugh uproarious, at the shrimp's little jig,
As the reef becomes a stage, for a strike of whimsy big.

In this underwater theater, with fins and tails so bright,
No one cares who's the star, everyone's a delight!
So join in on this dance, let your worries unfurl,
And sway with all the fishes in their watery whirl.

Reflections on a Sea of Calm

The mirror on the water reflects a silly scene,
Fish brush their scales with sunshine, forming a glimmering sheen.
A moorish idol preens and poses, an artist with a brush,
'Look at me!' he giggles, amidst a smiling hush.

Underneath the surface, a crab holds quite a show,
Pinching at the laughter, he sways to and fro.
A turtle floats on by, with a grin wide and big,
'What's so funny, my friends? Oh, just living the gig!'

An army of tiny shrimp puts on a conga line,
Dancing to the rhythm, in tune with the brine.
And while bubbles tease the coral, tickling fish with glee,
The laughter forms a current, set free in the sea.

So lean back in the current, let the laughter flow wide,
In the depths of joyful silence, let whimsy be your guide.
As you watch the world beneath, in a bubble-wrapped dream,
Remember that the ocean's heart beats to a whimsical theme.

Beneath the Surface: A Prelude

Beneath the waves of laughter, where the fish kin do dwell,
The underwater symphony plays a buoyant spell.
A fishy little opera sings of seashells and snails,
While a grouper drifts along, narrating grand tales.

Oh look at that old crab, with a fiddle-legged dance,
He clumsily poses, never missing a chance.
'I'll catch the finest seaweed, for my dinner tonight!'
But his friends all chuckle 'Dude, you're losing your bite!'

A slow-moving sea cucumber, with dreams of being fast,
Tripped on a sea lily, oh, such a funny blast!
The urchins all erupted, in soft collaborative cheer,
'We prefer you a slowpoke, our gently rolling dear!'

So come join in the merriment, as the tide sets the pace,
With a flick and a flip, meet your bubbly grace.
Beneath the surface chaos, find the hearts at play,
In the laughter of the fishes, where they brighten the day.

Surrender to Azure Calm

Bubbles rise like giggles, a fish in a hat,
Glimmers of laughter where sea turtles spat.
Coral grows gossip, with colors so bright,
While clams keep on whispering all through the night.

Seahorses tango, a peculiar sight,
With crabs doing cha-cha, oh what pure delight!
The starfish flexes, its arms in a twist,
As the octopus winks, can you say he's missed?

Jellyfish float by, like balloons on a spree,
Tickling the anemones, oh such glee!
While dolphin comedians joke 'till they snort,
In this underwater realm, laughter's the sport.

So dive in and dance with the bubble parade,
In this wacky blue world, no plans need be laid.
With giggles and splashes, we're out here to play,
In azure delights, come chase worries away.

Episodes of the Silent Deep

In depths where the fish dream, there's tales to be told,
Of a clam who found pearls that were shiny and bold.
A crab with a cane struts around with great flair,
While sea cucumbers just lounge without care.

The blowfish inflates, looking quite round,
Making faces at seahorses circling around.
The anglerfish grins with its light all aglow,
While grumpy old grouper just huffs and says 'No!'

One day a pod of dolphins appeared,
With jokes so absurd, they left fish in deep fear.
'Why did the seaweed not share all its snacks?'
'It was too close to shore, and the tide had some hacks!'

Yet in these great depths, the laughter won't cease,
For currents of joy bring a whimsical peace.
So join in the fun, take your fins for a spin,
In the silent deep ocean, let giggles begin!

A Glossary of Gentle Waves

Wave one: a tickle from a friendly fish fin,
Wave two: a splash that brings giggles within.
Wave three: a current with a flow that's just right,
Wave four: the ocean's laughter, echoing bright.

Driftwood drumming beats on the sandy beach floor,
While crabs write their tales in a soft, salty lore.
Sandy shoals giggle, as the turtles glide by,
With a wink and a wave, just to say 'Hi!'

A poetical dolphin, with a flip and a swish,
Composes a sonnet that vanishes with a swish.
'Ode to the seaweed,' it starts with a plea,
And ends with a chuckle, 'Now please, let me be!'

So venture with glee through this playful wet tome,
Where laughter's the language, and bubbles feel home.
In a glossary made of dance, song, and cheer,
The gentle waves gather, forever sincere.

Tides of Lasting Serenity

In the tides of calm, where silliness thrives,
The fish put on hats and play leapfrog dives.
An octopus teacher shows styles aplenty,
While shrimps form a band that sounds far from flashy.

The coral gossip grows, with whispers and laughs,
As the echinoderms draw up their funny graphs.
A dolphin named Chuckle plays hide and seek,
With giggles that echo all through the week.

Stingrays in costumes glide by with a spin,
Each one with a grin and a colorful fin.
While sea turtles ponder, with wise wide-eyed looks,
Rolling with laughter, they're writing the books.

So sail on these tides where joy's always near,
In a world filled with chuckles, no need for a seer.
With waves of fresh giggles and remedies to share,
Embrace the delight—float away without care!

Songs of the Blue Sanctuary

In the ocean deep, the fish do play,
With bubbles and giggles, they dance all day.
A crab in a top hat, quite the sight,
Twirls with a starfish, oh what a delight!

A dolphin sings, with a splash and a flip,
While turtles join in with a graceful dip.
Seashells applaud with a gentle clap,
As a clownfish tells jokes while taking a nap.

An octopus juggles, all eight arms in show,
While seaweed sways, putting on a glow.
The sea cucumbers wiggle with glee,
In this vibrant party, hang out by the sea!

So let's dive in, let's give it a whirl,
In this watery world, where laughter will swirl.
With fins and gills, we'll join in the cheer,
In the joyful depths, there's nothing to fear!

A Dance of Petals and Fins

Bright corals bloom in hues that amaze,
As the fish start a waltz in a watery daze.
A goldfish in slippers glides with a sway,
While seahorses tango, stealing the play!

Anemones giggle, their tentacles sway,
As the hermit crabs prance in their own little way.
A starfish spins tales, with five-pointed flair,
While jellyfish float without a care.

Bubble-blowing puffers compete for a prize,
In a contest of cuteness, oh what a surprise!
As the sunbeams laugh and cast a gold sheen,
The laughter of currents, a comedic scene.

So let's join the dance, jump in with no fear,
In this underwater ball, joy is so near.
With splashes and giggles, we'll whirl like a fin,
In petals and laughter, let the fun begin!

The Calm of a Liquid Garden

In the garden below, where the seaweed blooms,
Nemo tells stories that lighten the gloom.
A snail with a monocle, reading a book,
Says, "Join me for coffee, or take a quick look!"

The sea urchins chuckle, spiky and round,
While fishes in bow ties swim all around.
A clownfish in sneakers bounds like a pro,
With a shimmy and shake, putting on quite the show!

Seagrass waves gently, a soft serenade,
As the hermit crabs march in grand parade.
An orange anemone steals the limelight,
With a twist and a shout, it's pure delight!

In this liquid garden, no worries in sight,
Where joy is abundant, and the future looks bright.
So let's share some giggles, let our hearts twine,
In the calm of the depths, everything will be fine!

Shadows Among the Sea Glass

Underneath the waves, where the sunlight refracts,
Sea turtles tell secrets, oh how they relax!
A fish with a beard shares his wisdom of old,
While whispers of laughter through coral unfold.

The octopus ponders, with a curious wink,
As the sea stars gather to chat and to think.
"Oh, what's that bubbling? A party, we hear!"
Said the crab with a grin, "Oh, let's all get near!"

With lanternfish lighting up the jellyfish glow,
The dancing unfolds with a flow and a show.
A mermaid in flip-flops joins in the spree,
As sea urchins cheer, "Go, dance with glee!"

Among the clear glass, a mirage of cheer,
Where shadows would giggle, there's nothing to fear.
Let's dive into laughter, ride waves full of zest,
In this shimmering kingdom, we're all truly blessed!

Harmony Among the Fishes

In the coral, a clownfish grins,
Swapping tales of ocean sins,
A crab taps dance in a sideways way,
While sea cucumbers loaf all day.

A tango between a snail and a snail,
Each one trying not to fail,
The fish laugh, bubbles in the air,
As the seaweed sways without a care.

A dolphin whistles a silly tune,
Hoping to charm a passing moon,
But the octopus, with eight arms wide,
Joins the party, full of pride.

In their world, every splash is fun,
Life moves slow, no need to run,
With jellies dancing, colors bright,
Each wave a giggle, pure delight.

Lullaby of the Ocean Floor

Down below, where the seaweed grows,
A starfish hums with a gentle prose,
While shrimp tap feet like tiny shoes,
Creating rhythms, sharing news.

Anemones sway as they softly sway,
Inviting fish to dance and play,
With the echo of bubbles, a soft croon,
Bringing lullabies beneath the moon.

Sand dollars dream, not a care in sight,
While seahorses try to take flight,
Each wave whispers secrets old,
In this underwater realm, tales unfold.

Sleepy turtles nod off in glee,
As gentle waves go tickling thee,
Crabs sing softly, feeling bright,
In this dreamland, all feels right.

Ballet of the Gentle Currents

A shark pirouettes, quite out of place,
While the fish just giggle at his grace,
A seahorse twirls like it's on a string,
As jellyfish float, a circus ring.

Clownfish break dance, flipping around,
With the waves as music, profound,
Turtles drift, with a relaxed flair,
A slow-motion dance, without a care.

Starfish try to clap their arms,
While eels wiggle to their charms,
An orchestra of gurgles and swishes,
In this ballet, every creature wishes.

When currents change, the dance grows wild,
It's a party for each sea child,
With fins and flippers, all in sync,
In this aquatic waltz, they never blink.

Echoes of an Undersea Dream

Bubbles rise like giggles in blue,
A dolphin's laugh, the best cue,
With every echo, a burst of fun,
As the bright sun dips, day is done.

Corals chuckle as fish swim by,
Each wave a wink, a playful sigh,
The narwhal tells fishy jokes,
While sea turtles share silly pokes.

Anemones whisper to crabs and snails,
"Who's got the best underwater tales?"
They trade tall stories as giggles flow,
In this dreamland where laughter glows.

As night descends, a lull sings clear,
Dreams of bubbles bring endless cheer,
With winks and swirls, the ocean beams,
In these depths, all life smiles in dreams.

www.ingramcontent.com/pod-product-compliance
Lightning Source LLC
Chambersburg PA
CBHW070310120526
44590CB00017B/2619